THEY DIED TOO YOUNG

MARC BOLAN

BY

Tom Stockdale

This edition first published by Parragon Books Ltd in 1995

Produced by
Magpie Books Ltd, London

Copyright © Parragon Book Service Ltd 1995
Unit 13–17, Avonbridge Trading Estate
Atlantic Road
Avonmouth
Bristol BS11 9QD

Illustrations courtesy of: Rex Features.

This book is sold subject to the condition that it shall not,
by way of trade or otherwise, be lent, resold, hired out or
otherwise circulated without the publisher's prior consent
in any form of binding or cover other than that in which
it is published and without similar condition being
imposed on the subsequent purchaser.

ISBN 0 75250 694 3

A copy of the British Library Cataloguing in Publication
Data is available from the British Library.

Typeset by Hewer Text Composition Services, Edinburgh
Printed in Singapore by Printlink International Co.

In August 1994 the *Evening Standard* interviewed Noel Gallagher, songwriter with up-and-coming band Oasis. He said that, as all the great songs have already been written, the only thing left to do is rewrite them. His one admitted robbery was the guitar-line from T. Rex's 'Get it On' although, as he said, 'it doesn't belong to T. Rex . . . It's a blues riff'.

Rock's fine dividing line between borrowing and theft has specific relevance to Marc Bolan. His great influence in the tradition of the 'throwaway' world of the three-minute pop song is matched by the debt he acknowledged to various musicians, without whom he could not have carved an enduring niche in a small period of pop history. The fact that, over 20 years later, another musician was acknowledging him in the same way shows perfectly how Marc Bolan fashioned a new originality out of an existing form. As he said to *Disc* magazine in 1970, 'Let's face it, the majority of pop hits that make it are a permutation on the twelve-bar blues and I've found one that works.'

Admittedly, Bolan went through a pop wilderness, when the critics who had crowned him were just as ready to flay him. But at his death he was showing every sign of re-emerging into the mainstream, with his championing of the growing Punk and New Wave movements, and the tragedy of his death at the age of 29 is that of losing a man whose time was most definitely not over.

Childhood

Marc Bolan was born Mark Feld in London's Hackney Hospital on 30 September 1947, the second son of Simeon (known as Sid) and Phyllis Feld, who lived in the Borough. Sid was a lorry driver whose Polish-Russian father had been a Smithfield meat market porter and part-time bare-knuckle fighter. Phyllis' father was a greengrocer turned refuse-worker, and her mother was a domestic cleaner. They married in January 1945, and their first son Harry was born in June of that year.

Mark was named after one of Sid's brothers, who was killed in 1946 by a military camp policeman in Warwickshire in an act of drunken indiscipline. He was brought up in a happy family, in a world recovering from the war years aided by a rapid acceptance of American mass culture, and both boys lapped up a diet of radio and cinema, as well as comics and fairy tales. Audie Murphy was one of Mark's early heroes, and he was fascinated by the fear and excitement of horror movies, such as *Phantom of the Opera*. Phyllis' weekly job on a stall in Soho's Berwick Street market allowed her to provide them with some of the material glitter of the new age, but imagination was still the best toy box.

He was a popular pupil at Northwold Primary School, and although small for his age, he was always ready to take a leading role. He and Harry got on well, and as the younger brother, Mark quickly learned to act older than his age, and also to take older interests than might be usual; not many people would claim, as Mark did, that 'At nine years old I became Elvis Presley'.

His father had bought Mark a copy of Bill Haley and The Comets' 'See You Later Alligator', thinking that it was Bill Hayes' 'The Ballad Of Davy Crockett' – 'just one playing of that and I chucked Bill Hayes out of the window', said Bolan. The sound of rock 'n' roll, marked by Haley's 1956 leap into the charts with 'Rock Around the Clock', and the British rise of Elvis found Phyllis taking out a hire purchase agreement for a £9 acoustic guitar, which Mark received for his ninth birthday. Technical ability was not important, however, even when he joined a group that included fellow Northwold Primary pupil Helen Shapiro; simply owning the instrument, and standing like Elvis, was enough. Shapiro recalled that Mark's great asset was a quiff that covered his face when he combed his hair forward. Endless bedroom rehearsals were followed by gigs at a local coffee shop and a school, before a new school term split the band between their respective primary and secondary schools.

Another influence emerged in 1958 with Britain's answer to Elvis, Cliff Richard.

Mark did a fine impression of the teen idol, and claimed to have met Cliff at the 2i's coffee shop in Soho – there was also a story that he had carried Eddie Cochran's guitar at the Hackney Empire, where Mark went several times to be in the audience for the recording of the pop show *Oh Boy*, and where he would catch current pop favourites like Marty Wilde, Billy Fury and Adam Faith.

In September 1958 he started at secondary school, where he daydreamed his lessons away. An interest in words was still a long way from his mind, nor was he taken with the new realism of contemporary films like *Room at the Top* and *The Angry Silence*; his overriding obsession was with clothes. Although he had been impressed by the uniform of the Teddy Boys, he was more immediately struck by the 'non-uniform' of the Modernists. They used a constantly evolving style, adapting and combining garments in a creative and narcissistic way that Mark instantly understood.

His room was soon dominated by his clothes, and he would scour Hackney, and beyond into Soho, for shops and tailors who could satisfy his desire for originality but take into account his diminutive size. He later stated that he had always been a star, 'even if it was only being the star of three streets in Hackney'. By 1960, he was the leader of a local gang of like-minded friends who would meet and pose at halls and clubs, listening to successive hits from Elvis and Cliff, as well as Eddie Cochran's 'Three Steps to Heaven', and Ritchie Valens singing 'Tell

Laura I Love Her'. Jeff Dexter, a dancer friend of Mark's at this time, remembered him being both admired and hated by others who didn't have his strength of personality in wanting to stand out in a crowd.

Bolan agreed in a later interview, 'I was completely knocked out by my own image, by the idea of Mark Feld.' The expenses of his fixation were not small – 'I'd steal or hustle motorbikes to pay for them, clothes were all that mattered to me.' Mass raids on casual-wear shops were a regular part of the shopping experience, and the booty from them would be customized by Mark's mother to satisfy his individualist cravings. The term 'In-dividualist' was adopted to distinguish the style-conscious Modernists from the growing number who were becoming a more uniformed body, and would evolve into the Mods of the mid-sixties – Mark would probably have been impressed by the singular attitude of films like *The Hustler* and *The Misfits*, which could be seen at the cinema during 1961.

As a leading local Individualist, and probably also because of his relative youth, Bolan was one of three Stamford Hill teenagers interviewed by *Town* magazine for its September 1962 issue, under the headline 'The Young Take The Wheel'. His quick replies and photogenic looks won him lengthy quotes about bikes, shoulder-pads and keeping ahead of the crowd. The three mirrored the working-class politics of a generation who equated Conservatism with aspiration, despite the

Marc Bolan

The young Mark Feld was a fan of
Cliff Richard

reality of a shared bedroom in a 27-shilling-a-week flat in Hackney; 'they're for the rich, really, so I'm for them', said Mark.

By the time the article appeared, the Felds had moved to new council accommodation in London's Summerstown, between Wimbledon and Tooting, a colourless neighbourhood that left the Individualist right out on his own, probably feeling sympathy with the chart-topping hit of October, Roy Orbison's 'Only The Lonely'. By then, the lure of the West End was giving the 15-year-old the excitement he needed. The small boutiques and plethora of clubs were meeting places for the different youth cults, *Billy Liar* was sowing its flights of fancy from the big screen, and Mark found the clothes to fit him and the corners to pose in. He sometimes joined the scooter runs to seaside resorts which had become part of the fabric of weekend relaxation, and on one occasion ended up in hospital, after coming off a friend's bike on the journey to Brighton.

By 1962 the new wave of American-style music from artists such as Roy Orbison, Duane Eddy and Ricky Nelson, was coming over loud and clear on Radio Luxembourg; finding a place alongside them was Mark's former coffee-bar band co member, Helen Shapiro, whose light-weight pop hits, such as 'You Don't Know' and 'Walkin' Back to Happiness', gave him proof that it was possible to make ripples in a bigger pool. Shapiro was the headline act for a February 1963 gig in Bradford which had The Beatles placed fifth on the billing. Although music had not at that time been high on Mark's agenda, a viewing of Cliff Richard in *Summer Holiday* during that year provided the impetus for him to sing, more for the idea of stardom than of musicianship. Meanwhile, the emergence of The Beatles into the mainstream changed the emphasis of pop music from a singer to a singer/songwriter culture and would provide a more artistic and poetic outlet for any aspiring star.

Development of a Poet

Mark had left school at the earliest opportunity and without qualifications, and time fell heavy on his hands while the rest of his family was out at work. He began to read, and discovered a love for Greek myths and romantic poetry. When he signed on at the Labour Exchange he declared his trade as 'poet'. During this time, The Beatles had headed a revolution in the album charts, holding the number 1 spot for a year with *Please Please Me* and *With The*

Beatles. Film soundtracks like *South Pacific,* which had up to now held sway in the charts, would, for the most part, be kept out of them by the rock phenomenon – with the exception in 1965 of *West Side Story* and the forever popular *Sound of Music.*

Mark experienced a short period of employment as, simultaneously, a menswear salesman in Tooting and dish-washer at the local Wimpy. He soon retired to the family home, however, to continue reading. A more serious attempt at work was made when he persuaded his mother to pay £100 for him to enrol in a West End modelling school. He received at least two assignments, for the Littlewoods catalogue 1964-5, and a John Temple menswear brochure.

Mark had also taken to going to the studios where the children's television programme *The Five O'Clock Club* was recorded. He struck up a friendship with Allan Warren, one of its regular performers, and moved into a room in Warren's flat near Earls Court. During his six months' stay there, Mark discovered Bob Dylan, whose authenticity and individualism put him into a spotlight despite his obvious lack of playing skills. Dylan was one of only three pop artists who shared the number 1 album spot for the whole of 1965-6, the other two being The Beatles and The Rolling Stones. Elvis and Cliff were confined to the singles charts alongside Georgie Fame, The Kinks and The Hollies. Mark bought himself a harmonica, and would sit for hours, playing and talking himself

17

up – 'It was a full-time obsession', said Warren. They had the idea of getting Mark on Warren's television show, and booked a two-hour session in a studio, ending up with two songs, one of which, a version of Dylan's 'Blowin' In The Wind', was taken to A&R (Artists & Repertoire) at EMI. It received a polite refusal. A photographic session was done to accompany the tapes, but the television company wasn't interested. Nor were the other record companies that the pair visited over the next few weeks.

In the meantime, Mark's new domestic freedom allowed him to discover his sexuality. He was attracted to both sexes, and 'went to bed with anyone, because everyone did in those days', said Warren. Mark would look back on those days as a time of experimentation, feeling that he should 'try anything once', and would have been encouraged by the growing liberation reflected in cinema releases like *The Group* and *Repulsion*. There was an easy crossover with the gay scene in the area of clothing, and Mark's pretty looks won attention from both sides. However, his disappointment over the lack of interest in his demo tapes led to his return to Summerstown in spring 1965.

Meanwhile, Mark had also changed his name, firstly to Riggs, after a friend, Riggs O'Hara, an actor with whom he went on a trip to Paris. The excursion was turned into legend by Mark; he described a meeting with a magician in the Louvre, who invited him back home for a meal, and performed several displays of white

Marc would sometimes join the Mods on their scooter rides

Marc with June Child

magic. Mark's brother Harry heard a version which told that Mark found a slug in the hotel bath and came straight home. 'Mark could turn on the crap till the cows came home', said Jeff Dexter.

Back in the real world, and with another name change, this time to Toby Tyler, Bolan made friends with Mike Pruskin, who was working as a publicist for Van Morrison's Them, and who agreed to become his manager. They moved into a basement flat behind Baker Street, and while Mark played the guitar, listened to Dylan, read *The Hobbit* and wrote poem after poem, Pruskin dreamed up promotional schemes. Yet another change of name, to Marc Bolan, happened around the time of a big break, when the two managed to attract the attention of Jim

Economides, the American producer of
The Lettermen. He introduced Mark to
Decca's A&R man Dick Rowe, who had
rejected The Beatles, but had made amends
by signing The Rolling Stones. Rowe
offered Bolan his first recording deal on
9 August 1965, and sent him to a musical
director, Mike Leander. In September they
went into the studio and recorded three
songs, two of them originals; 'The Wizard'
(based on the Paris story) and 'Beyond The
Risin' Sun'. The recordings were given the
in-house orchestral backing treatment and
released with a publicity campaign, including television appearances on *Thank Your
Lucky Stars* and *Ready Steady Go!*, but the
single came to nothing. Some live dates
were played, but these only served to show
up Bolan's technical weakness and were
not successful.

Bolan may not have had instant success, but he was ready for it. He had become glamorously bohemian: suede boots, long jackets and curly hair replaced his previously lacquered Modernist style. Donovan, the 'English Dylan', had been signed by Pye Records, and the underground was moving towards the hippy movement which the American West Coast had spawned. Decca eventually brought out Bolan's second single in spring 1966, 'The Third Degree' and 'San Francisco Poet', providing a rockier sound and showing a more relaxed lyrical style, but this attempt was as unsuccessful as the first.

The lack of reward for their efforts got to Bolan and Pruskin, and when they had to do a moonlight flit from their flat with rent still owing, Pruskin decided to call it a day.

Marc needed another lucky break, and his meeting with Simon Napier-Bell suggested a new direction. Napier-Bell, a songwriter turned manager, saw the individuality of the young bohemian who had telephoned him out of the blue, claiming an instant sense of 'star quality'. He accepted Bolan's over-active imagination as part of an over-imaginative character; 'Marc was a wonderful, charming fraud . . . I just loved the voice.' Indeed, the voice had undergone a sudden and complete transformation from the overt Dylan copy to a quavering vibrato, punctuated with shrill bleating, that was truly original. An immediate studio session produced a demo that would eventually turn up on *The Beginnings of Doves* album of 1974, containing songs such as 'Hippy Gumbo' and 'Black and White Incident', and full of fractured images and references that worked through their sound rather than having any literal meaning.

Napier-Bell was managing The Yardbirds, who were already established when he took them on; the idea of taking and breaking an artist from scratch appealed to him, especially a 'personality' in contrast to the more serious musicians who made up The Yardbirds. He was interested in the recreational as well as the financial advantages of pop management, saying 'it was the modern equivalent of being the choirmaster, but in the sixties, instead of being arrested for the nasty little things you did round the back of the church, they gave you a million pounds and made you a hero'. Certainly there was a sexual aspect to his relationship with Bolan, even though Marc had a steady girlfriend in Terry Whipman. Napier-Bell considered Bolan to be more gay than straight, as there was more fun to be had on the gay scene, and Bolan always wanted to have fun. They chose 'Hippy Gumbo' as the single to launch the new-look Marc Bolan in November 1966, at a time when the Beach Boys were at number 1 with 'Good Vibrations'. Despite a negative record company reaction, Napier-Bell used his influence to force Parlophone into bringing the single out, and the resulting flop is now a very collectable item.

Napier-Bell had the idea of linking Bolan up with a noisy unmusical band of good-looking boys he had taken on in autumn 1966, called John's Children. They were

Tyrannosaurus Rex

John Peel was an early champion of
Tyrannosaurus Rex

one of the most intelligent and fun groups I ever met', he commented, 'but they weren't very good.' He put them into white suits, and left them to run wild during gigs. Marc was introduced to their singer, Andy Ellison, who liked his songs, and the guitarist was eased out to make way for a new band member. In this way, not only would Bolan get some lessons in performance, but John's Children would gain a songwriter.

Virtuosity was not the strong point of the band, but some single success in America had led to an album, and with Bolan incorporated into the group, Napier-Bell signed with Kit Lambert's Track Records, home to The Who and Jimi Hendrix. Their next release was to be the Bolan composition 'Desdemona', and a short tour of Germany was undertaken in April 1967 supporting The Who. At first Bolan would get drunk to ease his pre-gig nerves, but the other members quickly taught him how to be a 'nutter on stage'.

The tour turned into a competition of destruction, and Kit Lambert gave a final warning to Napier-Bell, because John's Children's unscripted rampages were up-staging the headliners. Seeing that the band were nothing without their perform-ance, Napier-Bell encouraged them. A Ludwigshafen gig was taken over by feed-back and audience chanting: Andy Ellison had dived into the crowd, and Bolan was chain-whipping his guitar. A planned stage fight led to a riot, the bouncers responding with violent glee, and John's Children escaped backstage just before the water-cannon arrived. The Who's set was cancelled and John's Children were thrown off the tour, having lost £25,000 worth of equipment in the process.

'Desdemona' was released in May (while the Tremeloes' 'Silence Is Golden' rode the top of the charts), but was refused airplay by the BBC due to the line 'lift up your skirt and fly' – a reference, Bolan claimed, to a witch on a broomstick. Chart success certainly could not be guaranteed from pirate radio play alone, and although the BBC recorded a four-song session for *Saturday Club*, broadcast on 17 June 1967, Bolan had done his time with John's Children, and was ready for something else.

The Band Takes Shape

Melody Maker carried an advertisement on 11 June 1967, saying 'Freaky lead guitarist, bass guitarist and drummer wanted for Marc Bolan's new group. Also any other astral flyers like with cars, amplification and that which never grows in window boxes.' The hippy references implied the new direction Bolan had set for himself, though opinions differed as to how deeply he immersed himself in the culture. Drummer Steve Peregrine Took said, 'I guess for a while Marc was a good hippy. Like, we used to sit around and rap about what needed changing.' Tony Visconti was more pithy; Marc 'was a Mod dressed up as a hippy'. As with the other influences he absorbed, Bolan played the part well. Within a short time he had picked up a beaten-up acoustic guitar and was using the vocabulary of the scene, and drummer Took, the only successful candidate from the auditions, was an ideal partner.

Took was a year younger than Bolan, and changed his name from Steve Porter shortly after their meeting (the name is that of one of the central characters from Tolkien's *Lord of the Rings*). He was withdrawn enough for Bolan's ideas to be the dominant ones, and was long-haired, velvet-clad, and naturally inclined towards the hippy movement.

Bolan's 'Larry the Lamb' vocal style, mystical lyrics and individualist dress sense slotted neatly into the scene.

The new name, Tyrannosaurus Rex, was chosen by Bolan because he wanted to have the same effect on the world as the dinosaur had had. They recorded material that John's Children had used, as well as some new material, 'One Inch Rock', 'Sleepy Maurice' and 'The Beginning of Doves'. The Tyrannosaurus Rex sound was there immediately; Bolan's slurred vocal delivery, Took's bongo beat, and accompanying folk and Eastern instrumentation. Bolan struck up a friendship with John Peel, then a pirate DJ with Radio London, who took it upon himself to champion the band and its strange-voiced singer. Peel's last show for Radio

London included six Bolan compositions, and his move to *Top Gear* on the new Radio 1 carried his admiration for Tyrannosaurus Rex to a wider audience. Peel would also insist that the band played at the gigs that he DJed. Bolan had another ally in Jeff Dexter, who was now also a live DJ. He had heard of Tyrannosaurus Rex, but did not know that Marc Bolan was Mark Feld until the two Mods-turned-hippies met face to face.

There was no room for Simon Napier-Bell on the hippy circuit; gigs were booked without a manager, and the anti-commercial phase of Bolan's career saw him actually bargaining venues down on their proposed fees. The charts were full of love, with Scott MacKenzie's 'San Francisco', and The Beatles' 'All You Need Is

Love' setting the tone for aspirant popsters.
Napier-Bell faded from Bolan's life. Also,
Track Records rejected a session that
Bolan did with Joe Boyd, who had
worked with Pink Floyd and the Incred-
ible String Band, and Bolan was forced to
look for a new record company, managing
to get his publishing company, Essex
Music, to pay for the studio time.

Meanwhile John Peel had arranged for
Tyrannosaurus Rex to appear on *Top
Gear*, and five songs were broadcast on 5
November. There was a re-broadcast
several weeks later, and Bolan passed a
selection panel for further sessions.

A couple of months before the *Top Gear*
session, Tony Visconti saw Tyrannosaurus
Rex at UFO, a leading underground venue.

Visconti had come over from the United States as an assistant to Procul Harum and Moody Blues producer, Denny Cordell, who had a close relationship with Essex Music in the Regal Zonophone company, and spent some of his time scouting for new bands for the label. He was impressed by 'this strange little person seated on the floor singing in what I thought to be something other than the English language', and left his card with Bolan.

The next day, Bolan and Took played for Visconti and Cordell, who said 'I don't understand them at all, but we'll sign them as our token underground group'. With a recording budget of £400 they spent four days in Advision Studios on an eight-track recorder. Most of the songs were old ones, although 'Debora', which was chosen as

34

the first single in April 1968, was one of
Bolan's most recent compositions. Its
clever simplicity, assisted by more *Top
Gear* sessions, got the song to number
34 in the charts, in a month when Louis
Armstrong was holding the fort with
'What A Wonderful World'. Single success is in itself promotion for an album, and
'My People Were Fair And Had Sky In
Their Hair . . . But Now They're Content To Wear Stars On Their Brows' (a
record-breaking 20-word album title) was
outselling Pink Floyd and Jimi Hendrix by
the end of July. It was an ideal hippy
album, full of fantasy figures and non-
materialist leanings; 'do not adjust your
sets', said the *New Musical Express*.

An increasing media profile and industry
connections got the band a place in the

Marc Bolan with Mickey Finn

Marc put everything into his stage
performances

Blackhill Enterprises management company, where Bolan met 26 year-old June Child, one of its employees. It was love at first sight, and Bolan's relationship with Terry Whipman came to a sudden halt. June left her partner, and the two quickly settled into a flat in Ladbroke Grove. She became a vital organizing influence in Bolan's life, taking care of the business and exploiting the many music business contacts she made through her work at Blackhill.

June's presence allowed Bolan's musical Romantic phase to flower. He would discuss his creativity with, and leave notes to, a muse called Poon, a fairy on his mantelpiece, and became aware of the writings of Kahlil Gibran, a Lebanese mystic and hippy guru. The summer of 1968 brought a follow-up single, 'One

Inch Rock', taken from the second and shorter-titled album *Prophets, Seers and Sages the Angel of the Ages*. The format remained the same, retreating into innocence, although with more of an Eastern element, and the concerts Tyrannosaurus Rex played were gatherings of the flower children, during a time when Simon and Garfunkel were impressing the record-buying public with their *Bookends* album. The Tyrannosaurus Rex concerts also provoked the establishment of a fan club in February 1969, as Bolan's looks attracted a growing female audience.

March 1969 saw the publication of *The Warlock of Love*, a collection of Bolan's blank verse which took him into the Pop Poet arena. The unconnected images and use of words for their sound over and above their meaning didn't work as well without the webbing of music, and there was no possibility of his being equated with Leonard Cohen, for example, who had been a published poet before he hit the musical spotlight. Also, by the time *The Warlock of Love* came out, the full-time hippy culture was beginning to break up, and musically, rock was creeping around the soft edges of the Romantic dream, implied by a battle at the top of the charts between *The Best of The Seekers* and Cream's *Goodbye*.

Prophets, Seers and Sages had kept the thin sound of the first album, but its sales did not match those of *My People Were Fair* . . . Other acts were moving in on the new tide, amongst them David Bowie, who had floated around the same scene as Bolan. In 1966, Kenneth Pitt, Bowie's manager, had

been in two minds over which of the two
young hopefuls he should take up with. By
June 1968 Bowie was attracting attention
at the bottom of a Royal Festival Hall bill
on which Tyrannosaurus Rex featured
prominently but less favourably. Bowie
also supported Tyrannosaurus Rex at several gigs through February 1969, when
Fleetwood Mac were enjoying their first
number 1 hit with 'Albatross'. Bolan's next
single, 'Pewter Suitor', failed to maintain
the success of the last two releases, and
there seemed to be a certain lack of
direction as the release date of the *Unicorn* album approached.

Unicorn was brought out in May, a week
before Dylan's *Nashville Skyline*, with
more John Peel sessions and on-air interviews, bringing accusations of financial

The flamboyant star

interests on the part of the DJ. Of course, any adverse reaction to the strangeness of the music only made Peel play the band even more. The single release 'King Of The Rumbling Spires' had evolved a rockier sound, which, with its use of piano and full drum-kit and Visconti's thickening production sound, helped the album to number 12 in the charts, ten places behind ex-label-mates The Who and their rock opera *Tommy*.

In August 1969 Tyrannosaurus Rex set off on their first tour of America. Unfortunately, the New York dates coincided with those of the Woodstock festival, and the city was empty of potential fans. The rest of the tour failed to give Bolan the impact he was hoping for, and although he made useful contacts, most memorably with singers Howard Kaylan and Mark Volman from The Turtles (who were the first to describe Bolan as a 'Cosmic Punk'), he returned to Britain without the break he had been expecting. He also returned without Steve Peregrine Took, who had spent much of the tour on acid, and had become increasingly unpredictable on-stage. Took's drug habits had always been a part of his life, but by now the former had begun to interfere with the latter.

In October Bolan advertised for a 'gentle guy who can play percussion . . . some bass guitar and vocal harmony'. The 300 replies never even got looked at, because through Pete Saunders, the photographer for *Prophets* and *Unicorn*, Bolan had already met Mickey Finn.

Approaching The Big Time

Three months older than Bolan, Finn had been through art college, a model agency and mural-painting, had a similar look to Took, and got on well with Bolan. They had a break in Wales to allow Finn to learn the material for the next album which Took had started, and to rehearse for a short tour in November.

The live shows brought out some of the leanings towards the electric sound which

Bolan had been experimenting with, and performances on *Top Gear* and John Peel's *Sunday Show* indicated his awareness of the growing status of the rock guitar-hero which would help Led Zeppelin and Black Sabbath to the top of the album charts in 1970.

Bolan was responsible for the guitar-line on Bowie's 'Prettiest Star' single, recorded during a 23rd birthday session in January 1970. Bowie also had a publishing deal with Essex Music, and had started working with Visconti. Bolan and Bowie used to encounter each other at Visconti's flat, and Bowie was said to acknowledge Bolan's single-minded attitude as an influence, although there was a keen rivalry between them.

Bolan also did some recording with Mar-
sha Hunt, star of *Hair*, who was working
with Visconti. She and Bolan found an
immediate attraction and began an affair.
Four Bolan originals were released by
Hunt, with Bolan himself appearing on
another of her singles. The affair was
discovered and put to an end by June
Child; the upshot was that on 30 January
1970, Marc and June got married in a small
registry office ceremony.

The album *A Beard of Stars* was released in
March 1970, and reached number 21 in
the charts, at a time when Simon and
Garfunkel's *Bridge over Troubled Water*
effortlessly held the pole position. It was
the first Bolan album to include electric
guitar, and Steve Took's parts had been
replaced by Mickey Finn's. The sound was

less cluttered, and two instrumentals were included, although most of the songs were a development of previous work.

Meanwhile in the same year Bolan was spiked with STP, a potent hallucinogenic drug, at a party for the British version of *Rolling Stone* magazine. He was sedated for several days and returned to earth terrified of a drug which he had only tried a couple of times. He claimed that the writing of 'Ride a White Swan' was the immediate result of the experience, although the two events were several months apart.

The song bristled with potential – a commercial song with the right production, released to a public which was ready for it. The band's name was abbreviated to T. Rex, and the single was brought out on

Great trousers!

A shot for the cover of T. Rex's *Greatest Hits*

a new label, Fly. A British tour was organized, and guaranteed to sell out with ticket prices held at the equivalent of 50 pence. Meanwhile there was a first appearance on *Top of the Pops*, and the addition of bassist Steve Currie, and The Turtles' Howard Kaylan on backing vocals towards the end of the tour in December. Steve Currie had begun his musical career in a jazz band, and slotted easily into the band after a successful audition in November.

December brought the release of the first album under the new name, called simply *T. Rex*. Its balance was more commercial, and it included several rock 'n' roll tracks which showed off Bolan's increasing ease with the electric guitar. It also featured two symphonic excerpts from a proposed concept album, *The Children of Rarn*, narrating a battle between good and evil, a project which bubbled up at intervals over the next few years. 'Ride a White Swan' took Bolan to number 2 as part of its 20-week stay in the top 50 (kept out of the number one spot by Clive Dunn's 'Grandad'), and *T. Rex* reached number 13 in the album charts at a time when the top-seller was Andy Williams' *Greatest Hits*. The all-important follow-up single was a simply structured twelve-bar called 'Hot Love', which hit number 1 after a month and stayed there for six weeks. Marc Bolan had hit the big time.

Ascent and Descent

T. Rex's final line-up was settled with the addition of drummer Bill Legend. Born Bill Fifield in May 1944, he had been through a number of bands in the 1960s, and was invited to sit in on the 'Hot Love' session by Tony Visconti. The success of the single prompted Bolan to look seriously for a drummer, Legend was invited to the auditions and was accepted. His first gig was in March 1971 in Detroit, on a five-week tour which was intended to capitalize on the exposure that Tyrannosaurus Rex had gained in 1969, but which in fact met with a singular lack of success. During the hectic touring schedule, the band settled itself into a method of recording in short bursts, which was not only cheaper, but also gave a raw edge to the finished vinyl as a result of the band only learning the songs during their recording.

On his return from America, Bolan planned a British tour for May, and on it he introduced his audiences to the glitter and sparkle that announced a new movement in pop. The single which followed it, 'Get It On', was the second number 1 in a row, and the ideal up-front accompaniment to Glam Rock's celebration of artifice. Its emphasis on style caused consternation amongst the 'authentic' rock critics, and arguments for and against T. Rex's 'sell-out' circulated throughout the music press. These were helped by Bolan's ability to give good copy himself, together with the fact that his name now sold papers. He saw himself as an artist moving away from preconceived notions of the rock form in a similar way to Dylan's famous move from the folk aesthetic to the electric guitar.

Bolan's public image was important to his newsworthiness. His up-market move to Maida Vale, the purchase of a white Rolls Royce, and his clubbing amongst the royalty of rock fuelled criticism as much as it fanned fervour in the growing teenage following which had taken over from the fans of his hippy period. John Peel was one of the victims of Bolan's ascent; he was ignored from the moment he decided not to play 'Get It On', which he considered unworthy of airplay. By this time, Bob Harris had taken over as presenter of *Top Gear*; he considered the 'new' Marc Bolan an exciting musical force.

Bolan's success was immediately reflected in his bargaining power in any contractual discussions. A renegotiation with Fly Records was negated a day later by Tony Secunda, who rang Fly to tell them that he had taken over as Bolan's manager. He had launched The Moody Blues and The Move, and had an aggressive management stance which Bolan liked. The resulting deal cut out Fly Records in favour of EMI's formation of the T. Rex Wax Co. label, with separate leasing

The Sweet

Gloria Jones

deals for other markets around the world. These deals made about $6 million in six months, and saw companies desperate to have a piece of T. Rex passing over cash in suitcases. 'We had great fun doing it', said Secunda.

Fly was still the label of release for *Electric Warrior*, the first album for the four-piece T. Rex line-up. It appeared in September 1971, a month before the start of a British tour which coined the phrase 'T. Rextasy', and saw the wrecking of three tour vehicles at just one gig by mobbing fans desperate for souvenirs, the most prized of which was a lock of Bolan's hair. *Electric Warrior* flew to number 1 in the album charts, and was in the top five of that year's best sellers. Its simple anthems and quirky song titles were snapped up by the teenage audiences who had become T. Rex's fan base, and 'Jeepster', one of its most memorable tracks, was only stopped from being the third number 1 in a row by Benny Hill's 'Ernie'. Bolan had become the successor to The Beatles in terms of audience hysteria, and police escorts were required before and after each concert.

Bolan did some more work on *The Children of Ram* before the October tour, but the schedule of tours and interviews gave little time for studio work. Meanwhile the December release of 'Get It On' in America saw Bolan looking at his first US number 1, and rumoured worldwide sales of 14 million.

The distinctive T. Rex sound was consolidated over the next few months with

'Telegram Sam' and 'Metal Guru' both reaching the top of the charts, while the compilation album *Bolan Boogie* joined them. The titles gave the songs a strength of identity which was both memorable and idiosyncratically rhythmic.

In February 1972 the band went to America to capitalize on their single success. But headline status and a cover-spot on *Rolling Stone* did not win over an audience with higher expectations than the teenage British fans – in fact there was greater support for technically proficient bands lower down on the bill. Further, Bolan's recent introduction to cocaine got him into trouble at a prestigious Carnegie Hall gig, when he set the volume at an inaudible level and fell over during the first song. Tony Secunda took off to Acapulco, telling Bolan that he had finished as manager. And certainly he was long gone by the time of the Wembley concert in March, which was filmed by Ringo Starr's Apple Films for the *Born to Boogie* film, and offered celluloid proof of the 'Bopping Elf' at his peak. With a short but sweet number 1 slot for the re-released double set of *My People Were Fair* and *Prophets, Seers and Sages*, Bolan was the first artist to have three number 1 albums in the UK in the same year.

By now the Glam Rock movement had taken on more players: Rod Stewart, Bowie, Elton John, The Sweet, Slade and Gary Glitter made Bolan the head of a movement. The fans dressed like their idols, and the concerts became as much fancy dress as musical entertainment.

Marc and Gloria with Rohan Rohan

Competition was rife and T. Rex's speedy recording methods were brought into play for the next album, *The Slider*. The album appeared in July, after some live dates, and reached number 4 in the charts, although sales tailed off quite abruptly. It was slated as 'close to an artistic collapse' by the music critic Charles Shaar Murray, but defended by Bolan as his first personal album, and a successful portrayal of the artist attempting to come to terms with changes in his life. Such changes included Bolan's taking over of the management of his company after Tony Secunda's departure, and progressively more of his time was spent dealing with his business affairs.

At this stage there were a number of departures from the Bolan camp; opinion was that he had started to believe his own publicity material, and posing had taken over his private life. Real privacy was hard enough to maintain, especially after his address was printed in a national newspaper, forcing him to retreat to a well-defended flat behind Marble Arch. A new adviser was recruited in the form of Tony Howard, who organized an injunction against Track Records to prevent them releasing the *Hard on Love* collection of demos which Bolan deemed unacceptable. The Track Records album would come out two years later as *The Beginning of Doves*.

Bolan was then able to turn his attention to the *Born to Boogie* project, which interspersed concert footage with fantasy scenes, and a star jam session with Ringo Starr and Elton John.

Before the film's December release, T. Rex took on America again. Despite their US label's television campaign, the band was obliged to let the Doobie Brothers take the top of the bill, as a result of bad reviews, and for the New York concert Bolan recruited three backing singers, including Gloria Jones, a Motown songwriter and member of the *Hair* cast, whom Bolan had met in England with the Joe Cocker entourage.

Returning home, Bolan promoted the September release of 'Children of the Revolution' (which went to number 2 in the charts) and inspected the thirteen-room vicarage that June had bought for them. She had stopped travelling with him, and was probably happier to let his increasing number of nights spent drinking be in her absence. Bolan's growing excesses were becoming noticeable, but were not comparable to Steve Took's; on 27 October Took choked to death on a cherry stone which stuck in his drug-numbed throat.

Just before *Born to Boogie*'s première on 14 December 1972 came the release of 'Solid Gold Easy Action': ten minutes in the writing, number 2 in the Christmas charts (behind Jimmy Osmond's 'Long-Haired Lover from Liverpool'). The film opened to packed houses, and two live London 'Rexmas' shows gave an up-tempo ending to the year.

The beginning of 1973 brought a number 3 slot for '20th Century Boy', but the *Tanx* album from which the single was lifted was over-heavy on technology and light on ideas. Similarly, the make-up of the cover photo did not hide the increasingly bloated features of the heavily drinking star. He was letting his image colour his perspective on the real world, and other Glam musicians were feeding the changing teenage market. 1973 was the year of Bowie albums with six different titles entering the charts, demonstrating that Bowie's changing image attracted fans in a way which Bolan could not manage. The Sweet, Gary Glitter and Slade all had number 1 singles during that year (with three for Slade), sweeping away Bolan's hope of dominating the teeny-bopper market.

By the summer of 1973, Bolan's affair with Gloria Jones was in full swing. She had become T. Rex's musical director during the last US tour, and the intervening months had brought them closer together. He was describing himself as a 'street punk', taking a lot of cocaine and drinking a lot of champagne, and obviously did not want the rural escape which June had provided. Gloria's musical abilities made her an apt consultant, and she had a busy professional life which gave her an understanding of Bolan's pop lifestyle. His next single, 'The Groover', reached number 4, and he announced that its successor would feature a totally new T. Rex sound.

A fourth American tour did nothing to break the band, although it gave Marc and Gloria plenty of time together. The rest of the band were not quite so happy. Currie and Legend were on £50 a week, and were increasingly disturbed by Bolan's erratic behaviour towards them. The American tour success of other British bands only made matters worse, although T. Rex did get 'Telegram Sam' and *The Slider* into the charts. Bill Legend got through a tour of the Far East and left the band in November. And by the time Bolan got back home, June had made up her mind to leave him.

Rebirth

Bolan emerged from the break from June with his curls cut off as if in rebirth, and he set up a flat in St John's Wood for himself and Gloria. As he planned the first British tour in 18 months, his *Great Hits* compilation struggled to number 32, with no hope of catching Slade at number 1. It appeared that he was losing control, and was not able to see beyond his 'star status'. Song production had become formulaic, and after arguments over royalty payments, Tony Visconti decided to call it a day. His last album with Bolan, *Zinc Alloy and the Hidden Riders of Tomorrow or a Creamed Cage in August*, was a co-production, and although it reached number 12 and offered lyrical features, it was out of step with the trends and fell out of the charts after two weeks. 'Teenage Dream', the single which accompanied the 'Truck Off' tour of January 1974, was seen as an attempt at a comeback in the eyes of a public who considered Bolan's era to have passed – something which Marc himself hadn't noticed. The 'new sound' of the tour and the 'Zinc Alloy' persona which Bolan had assumed was covered in the glitter which he had claimed he had finished with. It was clear to the critics that the band had not progressed, and the singles charts were more interested in artists like Mud, Suzi Quatro and Alvin Stardust.

For most of the rest of 1974, Bolan took a break from touring and recording. While Britain bathed in the shallow waters of the Bay City Rollers and Showaddywaddy, Bolan sipped drinks in the playgrounds of the world, with tax-healthy reasons for staying there – as he was not shy of telling the press during a brief stay in London. He did some producing for Pat Hall, Gloria's writing partner, and for her brother Richard, and played with some ideas for a new album. These songs and the best of those from the *Zinc Alloy* album, which had not been taken up by his American label, appeared as *The Light of Love* in the States. A September tour there saw a bloated Bolan parading his guitar prowess alongside the

Blue Oyster Cult and Kiss, and coming off much the worse for the comparison.

The single 'The Light Of Love' had been released in Britain, and was the first single since 'Ride A White Swan' not to make the top 20. The American album of the same name appeared with three new songs as *Bolan's Zip Gun* in February 1975, and failed to gain a chart position, despite the more contemporary sound of Gloria's Motown influence. The British market was more interested in melody, with Rod Stewart's 'Sailing' pointing the way for chart-hungry writers, and his album *Atlantic Crossing* making a matching chart pair. *Bolan's Zip Gun* was the last album to feature Mickey Finn, who left the band in February, prompting Bolan to comment that 'T. Rex no longer exists'.

Meanwhile, an indication of Bolan's singular lack of direction was his hopping between theme-album ideas, from the ever-present *The Children of Ram* and a 25th century 'teenage punkoid opera' called *Billy Super Duper*, to the growth of ideas for a work called *The London Opera*, which arose as a result of Bolan's return to a London base. This homecoming coincided with his first single success for 18 months with 'New York City', a 'boogie woogie mind poem' which got to number 15 in the charts and prompted a test-tour of four holiday resort towns. The tour found a more relaxed Bolan, chatting to the remaining fans and performing sets of the hits to interested holidaymakers, but it offered nothing new, and was seen as driftwood from the good ship Glam Rock.

There was a new development when television producer Mike Mansfield asked Bolan to appear on his afternoon pop show *Supersonic*. He recorded the first of them in September, during which time Gloria delivered a son they named Rolan, a self-confessed copy of Bowie calling his son Zowie. The television show was a vehicle for Mansfield's love of the older stars, and became Bolan's main public outlet. He also took up the offer of a thirteen-programme chat show from October, and although it didn't run its full course it put him in good spirits for the chances of his next record release.

The 'T. Rex Disco Party' single of that autumn only managed a number 30 placing, despite the catsuit and streaked hair that Bolan wore to promote it. The pomp of Queen's 'Bohemian Rhapsody' was ruling the airwaves, and T. Rex's proposed Christmas single, 'Christmas Bop', didn't even make it into production. After Christmas Bolan returned to profile-raising work. He was always good copy, even as a 'has-been', and a forthcoming tour was widely reported. It accompanied the new album, *Futuristic Dragon*, released in January 1976, and a single, 'London Boys', but it was no answer to Queen's *A Night at the Opera*. In spite of the tour, some isolated mobbing, and several good tracks on the album, the overall turnout at the gigs was poor, and album and single reached only numbers 50 and 40 respectively.

'London Boys' was part of Bolan's nostalgic return to his home town. The single was part of the *London Opera* idea, and he went back to the rock 'n' roll of his youth, even talking about heading a revival show. This immersion in the music of his youth was double edged, however, especially with respect to his next single, 'I Love To Boogie'. Bolan claimed it took ten minutes to write, and it rewarded him with a number 13 placing, but suffered from being a close match with a 1956 Webb Pierce song called 'Teenage Boogie'. The Bolan song was burned in public by some rockabilly fans, and was only saved from a court appearance by Bolan engaging the services of a musicologist to explain the long history of the main riff.

The ongoing television work included a special for *Supersonic* in August called *Rollin' Bolan*, which was the final appearance with Steve Currie, the last remaining member of the original four-piece. Currie cast no more public shadows until his death in a car accident in Portugal in 1981. By the next T. Rex performance, on *Top of the Pops* in October, the band had a new line-up, with keyboard player Peter 'Dino' Dines, who had been with the band for a year, together with guitarist Miller Anderson, and a rhythm section of Tony Newman and Herbie Flowers. The song they played was 'Laser Love', a disappointing number 41, the band was the most proficient Bolan would ever have, but no one could match the popularity of Abba's 'Dancing Queen', which was on a six-week run at the number 1 spot.

By this time Bolan was developing an interest in the newest musical explosion, Punk Rock. His initial hostility turned quickly to approval of the class-based, style-less style of the movement. He saw the 'new wave' as beating against the establishment in the way he had done in earlier years, and the weight of his positive voice in the general approbation drew some of them towards him.

The results were seen on the *Dandy in the Underworld* album in the spring of 1977. A more minimalist sound could be found inside the monochrome cover, but this couldn't compete with the anger of the sounds he was emulating. Nevertheless, his stated role as the 'Godfather of Punk' was backed up by Siouxsie and the Banshees' version of '20th Century Boy', and Bolan took The Damned as support for the 'Dandy in the Underworld' tour. 'He saw me wearing a Bolan T-shirt in a music paper photo, and I think that did it', said Captain Sensible. The March tour featured a good mix of old and new T. Rex songs, and Bolan adopted a health regime, replacing alcohol and fatty foods with Perrier and grilled fish. The end of the tour saw the departure of Miller Anderson, however, and without a fanbase to warrant radio air-play, there was no upturn in record sales for the album, or 'The Soul Of My Suit', its accompanying single.

Bolan's drive towards stability continued with the purchase of a house on the Lower Richmond Road in East Sheen, though he was content to live out of packing cases. The final *Supersonic* in March was succeeded by a monthly column for the *Record Mirror* in which Bolan gave his opinions on music and the world. He also jumped at Mike Mansfield's proposal for a new television programme which would become the six-episode *Marc*. The series provided a platform for his songbook, and gave him the opportunity to feature new wave bands like Generation X, The Jam and Radio Stars – the group fronted by his John's Children vocalist Andy Ellison, as well as the more appropriate afternoon television pop acts.

The final programme of the series, and what would be Bolan's last public performance, climaxed with the first live pairing of Bolan and Bowie. After performing individual slots, they joined each other to sing a hastily written number called 'Standing Next To You'. The rendition collapsed in the most ironic way, with

Bowie missing his vocal cue, and Bolan tripping into his microphone stand and falling off the stage.

Despite the final embarrassment, Bolan entered negotiations for a second series of the show for 1978, and into September was putting together a track list for a new retrospective to be called *Solid Gold T. Rex*. He was excited by the fact that some of his fans were organizing a 30th birthday event at Earls Court, and had volunteered to turn up and play a set. The early hours of 16 September guaranteed the cancellation of the celebration. Bolan had been at the Speakeasy Club to check out a new band, and went on to Morton's restaurant with Gloria and some friends. Leaving at about 4 am., Gloria and Marc drove off in her purple Mini 1275 GT, which was later found to have very low pressure in one tyre, and two loose nuts on another wheel. At about 5 am., the car crashed into a tree on a bend just past the hump-back bridge on Queen's Ride, on the southern edge of Barnes Common. Gloria was badly injured, trapped between the steering wheel and the seat. But the passenger side had taken the brunt of the collision, and there was no doubt that Marc Bolan was dead.

Four days later, Gloria was considered to be well enough to know the truth of the tragedy, and Marc Bolan's funeral was held at Golders Green crematorium, attended by a large crowd of family, friends, associates and fans.